ISBN 978-0-266-58997-6
PIBN 10871852

Comments

Clyde W. Kimball, Deputy Secretary

Louisiana Conservationist
ISSN 0024-6778
Volume 48, No. 3
Baton Rouge, LA 70808

M.J. "Mike" Foster, Governor
James H. Jenkins Jr., Secretary
Clyde W. Kimball, Deputy Secretary
Fredrick J. Prejean Sr., Undersecretary
John Roussel, Acting, Asst. Secretary
Johnnie Tarver, Acting, Asst. Secretary

Wildlife and Fisheries Commissioners
Glynn Carver, Many, Chairman
Perry Gisclair, Cut Off, Vice Chairman
Daniel J. Babin, Houma
Joseph B. Cormier, Lafayette
Jerald Hanchey, Lafayette
Edmund McIlhenny Jr., Avery Island
John F Schneider, Loranger

Division Administrators
Hugh Bateman, Wildlife
Al Carver, Acting, Information/Education
Bennie Fontenot, Inland Fisheries
William "Corky" Perret, Marine Fisheries
James Manning, Acting, Fur/Refuge
Winton Vidrine, Enforcement

Magazine Staff
Marianne Marsh, Editor
Maurice Cockerham, Information Manager
Andy Crawford, Staff Writer
Clifton Coles, Staff Writer
Jim Walsh, Staff Writer
Ula Simon, Circulation Manager

Copyright 1996 by the Louisiana Department of
Wildlife and Fisheries. This publication is not
responsible for unsolicited manuscripts, photographs
or other materials
    The Louisiana Conservationist is published
bimonthly except July/August by the Louisiana
Department of Wildlife and Fisheries, 2000 Quail
Drive, Baton Rouge, LA 70808, 504/ 765-2918.
Second-class postage paid at Baton Rouge, LA and
additional mailing offices. POSTMASTER: send
address changes to Louisiana Conservationist, P.O.
Box 98000, Baton Rouge, LA 70898.
    Regulations of the U.S. Department of the Interio
strictly prohibit unlawful discrimination in
departmental federally assisted programs on the basis
of race, color, national origin, age or handicap. Any
person who believes he or she has been discriminated
against in any program, activity or facility operated
by a recipient of federal assistance should write to:
Director, Office for Equal Opportunity, U.S.
Department of the Interior, Washington, D.C. 20240

This public document was published at an average cost of
$51,751.60. Approximately 45,500 copies of this document were
published at an average printing cost of $23,910.44. The total cost
of all printings of this document averages $23,910.44. This docu-
ment was published for Department of Wildlife and Fisheries,
2000 Quail Drive, Baton Rouge, Louisiana, 70808, by Harvey
Press, Inc., to provide information on outdoor opportunities in
Louisiana. This material was printed in accordance with the stan-
dards for printing by state agencies established pursuant to R.S.
43:31. Printing of this material was purchased in accordance with
the provisions of Title 43 of the Louisiana Revised Statutes.

A s Louisiana's water temperature begins to rise so does anticipation of the boating public toward another fun-packed season of waterborne activity. If you are like most Louisiana residents, more than 2 million strong, you will take to our waterways this summer as a recreational mariner. Regardless of the activity that lures us into a boat we all share a common label identifying us as the "Boating Public."

As Louisiana boaters, we carry on a long-standing tradition of taking to the water to elude regimented work schedules most of us endure in daily jobs. We use our rivers, bayous, lakes and streams as a haven to escape the clock and telephone. But, too often many of us forget that even recreational boating has associated risks that claim many lives and cause numerous injuries.

I recently learned that in 1995 Louisiana boaters filed several hundred accident claims with Louisiana insurance companies and that 39 deaths and 81 injuries occurred on our waterways. I was surprised to learn these figures accrued in spite of a vastly increased effort by our Department to educate boaters and rigidly enforce safety regulations designed to prevent marine accidents. So why the increase? Department experts point to several risk factors that have been amplified in recent years. 1)Louisiana has experienced an increase in the number of boats utilizing our waterways and boaters are concentrating their activities in limited geographic areas. 2)New user-groups, such as personal watercraft and performance boats, are operating in close proximity to traditional boaters and each can have conflicting use strategies. 3) Although this Department, along with the U.S. Coast Guard Auxiliary and the U.S. Power Squadron, has formally educated more boat operators than ever before, the total represents less than 20 percent of the boat operators on our waterways.

These factors, coupled with increased horsepower options on lighter hulls, have led to a dramatic increase in collision accidents in Louisiana and across the nation.

As Deputy Secretary of the Department of Wildlife and Fisheries and the steward of recreational boating in Louisiana, I have pledged full support to our boating safety program and the idea of creating a safe boating environment. I urge each of our citizens who participate in the boating tradition to become responsible boaters by taking a safe boating course and learning the rules and skills necessary to safely operate a boat. I ask that every boater exhibit common courtesy to every other boater, and that each respect the other's activity and presence. I remind you that operating a boat requires skill, common sense, good judgment and safe boating practices. Don't leave any of them at the dock!

LOUISIANA
Conservationist
CONTENTS

Pg. 18

Front Cover Gulf Fritillary
By Gary N. Ross

Back Cover Canebrake
rattlesnake *By Latimore Smith*

Next Issue *1996-97 Louisiana Conservationist Calendar*

Published by the Department of Wildlife and Fisheries in the interest of conservation of Louisiana natural resources.

CATCHING LOUISIANA Blues

BY MARIANNE MARSH

t's a hot, sunny, August day. Grand Isle State Park is full of people fishing, swimming, sunbathing and picnicking. It looks inviting and very tempting but our group is on a different mission — crabbing.

Imagine a family of three generations — four young boys, three parents, two grandparents — carrying 12 crab nets, two dozen chicken necks and a large ice chest. Up at the crack of dawn and out on the pier, everyone baiting nets, checking for crabs and generally having a good time.

crawl in. When the net is smoothly and forcefully retrieved, the two wire circles form a basket, trapping the crab in the bottom.

License requirements for crabbing varies with intent. Commercial crabbers must purchase a commercial crab license in addition to a crab trap gear license. Commercial crabbing is defined as 11 or more traps set in water. Crab traps for recreational use are defined as 10 or less traps and requires a recreational crab trap license in addition to a basic fishing license.

Dropnets do not require a license of any kind unless fishing from a boat or in a wildlife management area or refuge. In these cases a basic fishing license is required. On a management area or refuge a Wild Louisiana Stamp can be used in lieu of a fishing license.

There is no legal crab season, but peak time runs from midsummer to very early fall. Crabs are migratory and move into shallow, warm waters for mating. A female crab in the berry stage can easily be distinguished by the mass of eggs on the underside. Louisiana law requires that crabs caught in the berry stage must be returned to the water, whether caught by a commercial crabber or a recreational net. Possession or sale of these crabs is punishable by law. For additional information on Louisiana's fishing laws a copy of *Louisiana's 1996 Fishing Regulations* pamphlet can be obtained through LDWF, local sheriffs' offices or local sporting goods stores.

Catching crabs is easy and can be done from a boat, a pier, along the roadside or at the beach. Bait is usually chicken parts or fish heads, either of which is guaranteed to

Photo by Marianne Marsh

Constantly checking the nets will only produce empty nets and disappointed children. Keeping the nets undisturbed is one key factor to catching crabs. These children didn't have much luck as they checked their nets every few minutes.

Photo by Marianne Marsh

Patience and persistence will eventually pay-off, with an afternoon crab boil as the reward. Although it is enjoyed by all, it is the responsibility of the experienced crabbers to teach the inexperienced how to crack and eat their catch.

Photo by Marianne Marsh

attract crabs. Dropnets placed in an open waterway such as a beach or a roadside bayou require a float. Empty 2-liter plastic drink bottles make great inexpensive floats. Allow enough string from the float to keep the net flat on the water bottom. If crabbing off a pier, tie the net to the pier. If there is a strong current, add enough weight on the net or bait to keep it in place.

When crabbing in a popular spot be sure to mark your nets or floats so as not to disturb someone else's fishing. Never tamper with another person's nets or traps or remove crabs. Rest assured an arrest and a steep fine will follow if caught.

The object behind crabbing, obviously, is catching crabs. To do this, nets must sit in the water, undisturbed, for a reasonable amount of time — an extremely difficult task for children. I speak from experience. A child will not allow more than six or seven minutes to pass before pulling up the nets. Crabs are wise to nets. A lot of unnecessary action will only produce empty nets and disappointed children.

These blue crustaceans have a personality separate and apart from any other shelled animal. They're quick, smart and have a real attitude about being in a net. They can sidestep one in the blink of an eye. One method to avoid an empty net is to pull it up quickly, giving the crab no time to scurry off. Another way is to start slow, allowing the crab to stay with the bait. It's really a trial and error system. But once the net is extended, the basket prevents the crab from getting away — until it reaches land. When the net is flat again on the ground, that little blue creature is out of there. Children find this retreat maneuver of the crab somewhat exciting. As the crab scurries through their legs they'll jump up and down laughing and screaming at the same time. At this point, a scoop net is really handy.

Crabs are not only crafty and speedy, but very defensive. Their primary defense mechanisms are beautiful blue pinchers that display a natural, beautiful, blue and orange color that warrants

attention.
Beware, because
while admiring
the crab it will
launch an attack
on a finger, hand,
nose or anything
close by. A crab's
claws can clamp
down with
enough force to
draw blood. This
is a good time to
mention that
shoes are neces-
sary if crabbing
on a beach or
along the bayous.

LDWF photo

Photo by Marianne Marsh

*Live crabs can be
kept on ice (inset)
for about a day
without spoilage.
Once cooked,
whole crabs trade
their natural blue
color for a deep
reddish-orange.
Boiled crabs are a
favorite among
seafood lovers
everywhere.
It means good
eating and good
fun for everyone.*

Once the
crabbing is done
and the ice chest
is full, the feast begins. Live crabs can be
kept on ice without spoilage for about a day.
Keep them in a cool shaded area draining the
ice regularly. Cooking dead ones is acceptable only if they were recently caught. This
rule does not apply to crabs purchased at a
seafood market. Crabs purchased at a local
market should be alive. Dead crabs suggest
a long storage period. Cooking crabs that
have been dead for several days is a serious
health risk.

Next comes the backyard crab boil. A
good crab boil is rivaled by few backyard
barbeques. The boil is prepared much like a
crawfish boil, with spicy seasonings of
cayenne pepper, salt, onions, garlic, lemons
and a few inherited family secrets. Once
cooked, crabs trade their beautiful blue color
for a deep reddish-orange. They are then
ready to eat. Cover the tables with newspa-
per, pour the crabs across the table, sit down
and begin cracking. The only tool needed for
eating boiled crabs is a pair of crab crackers
for the claws (a pair of pliers or a nut crack-
er works great). The rest is done by hand.

When I was a young girl my family went
crabbing along Pass Manchac. I remember
hauling up nets, sometimes empty, sometimes full, and squealing as the crabs retreat-
ed back through my legs. Most of all, I
remember cracking and eating boiled crabs
until my fingers hurt. To this day I know few
people who can crack and eat as many boiled
Louisiana blues as my mother and I.

A social jaunt to Louisiana's coastal waterways for blue crabs can be an enjoyable and
fulfilling day. Go back to the group in the
earlier image: a long day on the beach, an ice
chest full of blue crabs, the aroma of hot crab
boil in the air, and the taste of fresh boiled
crabs still on the taste buds.

Mission accomplished.

Photo by Marianne Marsh

THE LOW-DOWN
ON
Louisiana's Specks

totalled an estimated 5.9 million trout. Then a severe freeze hit the marshes in December which killed millions of speckled trout and forced others to relocate to deeper areas including the open Gulf.

Although data indicate that many larger trout were able to escape the cold temperatures and survive, trout numbers still were depressed and harvest in 1984 plummeted to only 1.2 million.

This decline was short-lived, however. In 1985, harvest increased to about 4.7 million and by 1986 had peaked at a record high of just more than 10.5 million seatrout.

During the next two years, harvest dropped some but this was partly a reflection of a 12-inch minimum size limits imposed in 1987 and environmental conditions. The creel limit reduction to 25 fish per day in 1988 had an affect on catch by individual anglers, but did not greatly affect total harvest. The take during these two years still was comparable to 1983.

A severe freeze in 1989 began another cycle. Department of Wildlife and Fisheries samples showed predictable results — nearly all the trout captured immediately following the freeze were taken from the Gulf and the lower bays. Equally as predictable was the sharp decline in recreational catches, which remained low for a year (1990) and then began an upward movement.

Despite the kills during 1989, trout harvest the following year was higher (2.4 million) than the year after the 1983 freeze. This illustrates the uniqueness of each freeze and the dependence upon access to deeper water to buffer effects of extremely low water temperatures. The 1983 freeze involved a sudden, dramatic drop in temperatures followed by a prolonged freeze. The hard freeze in 1989 was preceded by sustained relatively cold temperatures. Because trout populations had time to adjust to colder water temperatures and move to deeper water, they fared better when freezing weather hit.

Harvest during 1991 shot up to more than 6 million specks and has fluctuated only slightly since that time.

The freeze in February of this year did not seem to set up a repeat of this cycle. One factor working in the favor of the seatrout fishery is that cold weather prior to February probably pushed many smaller specks into deeper, open water. It will, however, be a couple of years before effects of the three days of sub-freezing temperatures are known.

Anglers should know their catch does not necessarily serve as a marker of the health of trout populations. There are conditions under which catch is relatively low, not because of lower numbers of fish but because trout simply are not as readily available for harvest. Freezes can drastically influence distribution of fish long after the freeze and can have a major impact on overall fishing success for a significant period of time.

Salinities also play a huge role in where seatrout will be found during the summer spawning and fishing season. If salinities are high in the marshes, trout move closer to these nursery areas and easily can be found by anglers in bays and along beaches.

Low salinities in marshes, on the other hand, result in trout that are more often located in open Gulf water, making it harder for anglers to locate them. Flooding in the marshes similarly disperses trout. Lower harvest can be expected in the latter scenarios, even if trout populations are healthy.

To keep track of speckled trout populations, the LDWF Finfish Section was established in 1985 in response to recommendations by the Governor's Task Force on Saltwater Finfish Management. These recommendations also led to creation by the legislature of a new license for recreational saltwater anglers and a new seller's license for commercial saltwater fishermen. Act 295 of the 1984 Legislative Session further stipulated that proceeds from sale of the new

LDWF biologists keep tabs on speckled trout populations through sampling, using experimental seines and other nets.

licenses and other gear licenses required for taking commercial finfish would be be used to support research and management of saltwater fish species.

Comprehensive sampling by biologists from this section began in earnest in January 1986 and more than 1,700 samples have been collected and analyzed annually since that time. Experimental gill and trammel nets and seines are used conjunctively to gauge relative abundance, year class strength, standing crop and movements of various species including speckled trout. Sample sites are arranged to cover beach, mid-marsh and upper-marsh areas along the entire Louisiana coast.

From these samples and other data on the species and the fishery, age of fish and spawning potential ratio (which indicates spawning strength of a given population compared to estimated spawning potential of an unfished population) are determined. These data are used to determine if adjustments in regulations are necessary.

Spawning potential ratio (SPR) is one of the more common indexes in gauging the health of speckled trout populations in recent years: This figure indicates the number of eggs produced in a population being harvested as compared to an unfished population. Let's break that down into simpler terms. An SPR of 18 percent tells scientists

that if, for example, an unfished population produces 100 eggs, that same population would produce 18 eggs when harvest is occurring.

It has been estimated that an SPR of 16 percent is more than enough to ensure numbers of young spotted seatrout available to Louisiana anglers are not reduced. This level is based upon observations over a 13-year period which included several freezes and widely varying environmental conditions. Trout populations are considered healthy as long as the SPR remains at or greater than 16 percent. The population may be healthy at lower SPRs, but Department biologists prefer to err on the side of caution.

Where do seatrout populations currently stand on this scale? Estimates are that SPR is between 19 and 24 percent, depending upon some of the types of data used. It is easy to see that seatrout are not in trouble.

If speckled trout health is determined in great part by looking at the SPR, would it be better to try to establish a higher SPR? That depends on the goals of the fishery. If the goal is to harvest a lot of fish, you can't get a higher SPR. More fish removed from the fishery equals fewer eggs produced. If the goal is to catch larger fish and lower harvests are acceptable, then some upward movement of the SPR is possible. This means, however, that more fishermen will

search clearly that speckled 'vest can drop ly in response environmental but catch and st also moves ward as those tions improve.

a Conservationist

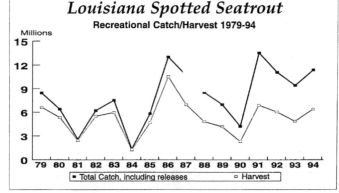

Louisiana Spotted Seatrout
Recreational Catch/Harvest 1979-94

Millions

Legend: ■ Total Catch, including releases   □ Harvest

have to release more fish (possibly many more fish) to increase the chances of catching bigger fish.

But SPR manipulation can affect a fishery's population only so much. In simple terms, only so many speckled trout can be supported by available habitat. If harvest of seatrout was ended today, the population could not grow forever. It would eventually reach a point where no more specks could survive. This principal of "carrying capacity" affects all living things.

Will the health of trout populations increase when the 1997 netting season is closed and commercial take is limited to rod and reel fishing? On the surface, one might

population. It will be a simple matter of increased availability. The difference between the number of fish previously taken by nets and the number commercially taken under the new regulations will be available for harvest by recreational anglers.

The bottom line is that Louisiana's speckled seatrout are not in trouble. There will always be years when Mother Nature intervenes and reduces the population. Nothing can be done about that.

Of course, there is another factor that seriously threatens availability of speckled trout. Erosion of valuable marshes, the ecosystem in which seatrout spawn, could drastically impact this and other marine species. These

Catches of huge trout, like this 8-pounder caught in April 1995, are indicative of the peak of speckled trout populations.

Photo courtesy of Andre LaFosse

expect to see a large increase in numbers of trout in Louisiana waters. Indeed, recreational anglers may find more fish.

What anglers should realize, however, is that the actual population probably will increase only slightly, if at all. One of two things are likely to happen. If the commercial harvest of seatrout remains the same in a hook-and-line fishery as under the current net fishery, recreational fishermen will not notice pronounced difference.

If the new regulations result in a reduced commercial take, what coastal anglers will be seeing is not an increase in the overall

important nursery areas are disappearing at an estimated rate of 25 square miles per year. As marshes transform into open bays, the food chain might change and the numbers of spotted seatrout could well decrease. We may not see the effects for years, but the potential harm to this recreational species certainly highlights the immediate need for protection and restoration of the fragile coastal marshlands of the state.

By keeping a watchful eye on the fisheries, however, Department biologists hope to ensure that our spotted seatrout thrive for years to come.

Brown snake

a Ground RATTLER?

STORY & PHOTOGRAPHY BY JEFF BOUNDY

There are two sure signs of spring in Louisiana — gardening and ground rattlers. One is a source of sweat and labor. The other is the cause of much trauma, fear and anxiety. I can't relieve you of your gardening, but I can eliminate your fear of the "ground rattler" with one word — harmless. In fact another word comes to mind regarding the little snakes — beneficial. The "ground rattlers" turning up in gardens every spring are usually brown snakes or earth snakes. Nearly every yard in Louisiana has these worm, slug, snail and

The true ground or pygmy rattlesnake (*Sistrurus miliaris*) is uncommon in Louisiana and prefers pine lands over suburbs. Occasionally a true pygmy rattler turns up in a yard, as one did near Baton Rouge some years ago. But, it was the only real ground rattler of more than a hundred such reports during the past 30 years from that region; the others were all harmless brown or earth snakes. Pygmy rattlers are usually 10-20 inches long, and very stout with a head much wider than the neck. As with other vipers, the pupil of the eye is etc. Placing a constricting band a few inches above the bite is optional, but it should not be tight enough to impede blood circulation. If medical treatment is more than 20 minutes away, and the bite is less than 10 minutes old, short, shallow incisions can be made over the bite. Some venom can be sucked through these incisions, but only if the mouth is free of open sores. After 15 minutes, the venom will have been absorbed and dispersed within the body tissues, and cannot be extracted.

What about other snakes that turn up in yards? Certain harmless snakes are thought to be copperheads, cottonmouths or rattlesnakes. The true copperhead, another viper, is a stout beige snake with a pink or orange tint and broad brown crossbands across the back. The head may be brown to orange, but has no markings. One snake commonly mistaken for a copperhead is the corn snake, which is a large constrictor that lives in pinelands. They are gray to bright orange with a row of brown or red blotches down the back. The head is marked with an orange or brown arrow-shaped band on top and another band through the eyes. The head is narrow and not much wider than the neck. The belly is white with alternating black blotches. Corn snakes often turn up in suburban areas and farmlands near forested regions, and feed on rodents.

The rat, or chicken snake, is another large constrictor that is dark brown with brown or black blotches down the back. It is white on the throat, but the underside becomes progressively darker towards the tail. The rat snake has the unfortunate habit of vibrating its tail, leading many people to believe that it's a rattlesnake. Despite their aggressive temperament, their bite is harmless.

"Water moccasin" is a generic term used for any dark colored snake in the water. Only one species of aquatic snake in the South is venomous — the cottonmouth or stump-tailed moccasin. Cottonmouths are large, stout-bodied snakes with a broad, chunky head. There is a sharp angle from atop the eye passing around the top of the snout. Like other vipers, the cottonmouth has vertical pupils and a large facial pit. Other aquatic snakes in Louisiana include eight species of water and crawfish snakes. Most of these are dark brown or black with vague markings similar to those of the cottonmouth. However, they possess round eye

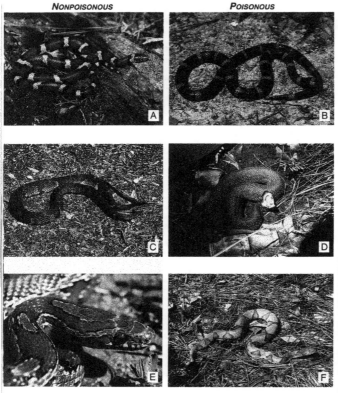

NONPOISONOUS	POISONOUS
A	B
C	D
E	F

Proper identification of snakes is of utmost importance. Many common, nonpoisonous species are often mistaken as dangerous and venomous and unnecessarily killed. The photographs above show the differences between several species often mistaken as poisonous: a)Louisiana milk snake and b) coral snake; c) banded water snake and d) cottonmouth (the cotton-white interior of the mouth gives the snake its common name); e) corn snake and f) copperhead. If a snake cannot be accurately identified, leave it alone. The majority of snake bites occur from attempts to handle or kill venomous snakes.

pupils, lack the facial pits, and lack the prominent ridge around the snout found on cottonmouths. If you can't identify the snake with certainty leave it alone; most snake bites result from attempting to handle or kill venomous snakes.

The coral snake has three mimics in Louisiana: the milk snake, scarlet kingsnake and scarlet snake. The famous rhyme, "red touches yellow, kill a fellow; red touches black, good for Jack" works for distinguishing the venomous coral snake from its harmless mimics. The basic color pattern of the coral snake is narrow yellow rings with a black band on one side and a red band on the other side of each ring. The harmless species have white or yellow rings bordered by black on both sides. Coral snakes are not found in swamps and are limited to dry pine or pine-hardwood forests east of the Amite River and in upland areas north of Lafayette and Lake Charles. Coral snake bites are neurotoxic, causing a shut-down of certain bodily functions. The danger of their bites is that they are often painless, so that symptoms may not become evident until too late. There is no first aid treatment for a coral snake bite except to get the victim to a medical facility as soon as possible.

Despite the presence of venomous snakes throughout Louisiana, most of our snakes are harmless, beneficial and interesting. After years of constant slaughter by uninformed people, harmless and venomous snakes alike are now being seen as an integral part of our natural heritage. Education alleviates fear, and proper identification of flower-bed snakes as well as other species will make gardening and other outdoor activities in Louisiana a little less worrisome.

PRIME TABLE FARE

STORY & PHOTOGRAPHY BY CHARLES W. FRANK

I guess nostalgia has a bit to do with our outdoor activities and sheepshead ring the bell for me. These feisty fighters are wide ranging, crafty and available all year. Bayous or open Gulf waters, shallow bays or rock jetties, oil platforms or pilings of long-demolished trapper's shacks all harbor their share of *Archosargus probatocephalus* — "sheepshead" to you less literate types and there are other nasty names for these bait stealing rascals. Their diet consists of hard shelled critters — barnacles, fiddler crabs, small blue crabs and other marine growth that their strong teeth crush with ease. Trying to get a hook out of those clenched choppers can be a chore. Their range is as extensive as their menu — from Nova Scotia to the Gulf of Mexico — but they seem to prefer the warm water of southern latitudes

when north winds roil the Atlantic coast. Despite their year round presence in Louisiana waters, the sheepshead is migratory. In the spring, adults swim offshore to spawn. That's when you can catch them under offshore oil platforms, their mouths green from feeding on marine mosses, in 12 to 15 feet of water. The young return to shallow grass beds until maturity. On the eastern seaboard they are considered prime table fare — but in Louisiana, many sportsmen consider them trash fish. This is changing, with the re-introduction of this striped rascal to the specialty menu in a number of better and more knowledgeable cajun chefs' repitoires.

Before Paul Prudhomme and blackened redfish, before trout almondine and trout Veronique, fine restaurants and hotels listed sheepshead. Old menus from the Gruenwald

Before Paul Prudhomme and blackened redfish, before trout almondine and trout Veroniques, fine restaurants and hotels listed sheepshead on their menus regularly.

Sheepshead can range from the smallest to monsters like this one, but they seldom do more than nibble. Even the largest are gentle feeders.

and Monteleone, Commander's Palace and Galitoires featured this choice of the elderly gourmet.

My first contact with sheepshead was with a ne'er-do-well uncle. He was the kind of guy every kid ought to grow up with. Unc never was a big success and, in fact, was sort of the black sheep of our family. Slightly overweight and balding, he wore the look of the downtrodden victim of hard times. But when fishing was the topic, his eyes would begin to twinkle and the cares and woes of making a living vanished. The Great Depression of the 1920s and 1930s was in full bloom and men like Unc had been beaten down. Even though times were tough, Unc never let work interfere with fishing, hence a succession of jobs. He was a natural artist at fishing and sheepshead were his favorite subject. He had refined the rig and technique and had no peers.

"Watch the tip of the rod son. Hold your finger under the line and you'll feel and see what those rascals are up to." Heck, Unc could think like a fish, and he knew how to get a kid's attention without being "adult" about it."Use enough sinker so you can hold the bottom and when the rod tip begins to twitch, gently hang back on that rod, and you've got him."

We'd catch a ride on a streetcar to the batture of the Mississippi River. The rattle of those wheels conjure up memories I never want to forget. Buying a hand full of river shrimp, Unc put them in an old wicker basket lined with cypress sawdust. Two small

chunks of ice kept the sawdust cool and moist and the shrimp alive. Streetcar fare was a nickel and you could get unlimited transfers around the belt. We'd climb aboard and head for the mouth of what was then the New Basin Canal (now a four-lane highway). Stopping at the last bridge to buy a bucket of clams, we'd head for the newly constructed Lake Pontchartrain sea wall and get off at shelter #2. I'd take a small hammer and crack the clam shells, tossing them into the lake, close to the sea wall. Unc would light up his first Picayune cigarette. As he exhaled his last drag of thick aroma-laden smoke , he'd hand me a cast net he'd knitted. "Okay son, time to pick up supper." The lake was pristine in those days and in half an hour we'd have half a bucket of beautiful shrimp to boil for supper.

By now the sheepshead were schooling on the remains of the clam chum, but Unc never believed in rushing nature. He'd light another Picayune and I'd shake out the cast net to dry. It was made with sea island cotton twine, not monofilament, and Unc wanted it to last. I think those Picayunes were the reason I never smoked and, incidently, why Unc died at a ripe old age and not from cancer. Heck, no one could smoke enough of those things to get in any trouble, especially if you mixed enough fresh salt air with the smoke. When Unc finished smoking, I could try for the sheepshead. We used a #4 or #6 short-shank O'Shaughnessy hook, stout but not too large, threading the river shrimp carefully to cover the barb. In another hour you'll be tied into a scrappy striped thief with a buck-toothed smile. You'll need a stout de-hooker or needle-nosed fishing pliers to get that hook out.

Best of all, you won't have to put a ruler alongside to decide if he's a keeper. Your only guide is your conscience as a sportsman. Catch and keep only what you need, and release the rest.

Like most of you, I have my share of game and fish cookbooks. Quite a shelf full in fact. Imagine my surprise to find no recipes for sheepshead. Oh, there were dozens of recipes for specks, redfish, mackerel, and pompano, but no sheepshead. Well, I called an old friend at Christian's Restaurant whose partner was a descendant of the Alciotores, proprietors of Galitoire's Restaurant in the New Orleans French Quarter. He graciously offered two of their old culinary secrets.

If you still can't catch sheepshead, use the sauce on an old pair of tennis shoes. You'll love them.　　　　　　　　　　　　　🐟

Place sheepshead filets in creole sauce and simmer for 15 minutes longer. You'll be a sheepshead fan from the first tentative taste.

Hollandaise Sauce

6	egg yolks
1	teaspoon red wine vinegar
2	teaspoons water
12	ounces melted butter
	salt and cayenne pepper to taste

Put egg yolks, vinegar and water in a bowl over hot water till sauce is thick and creamy. Do not curdle egg yolks. Add butter a little at a time in a small stream while beating. If too thick, thin with warm water. Season with salt and cayenne pepper to taste.

Variation: Cook the creole sauce until thick (about 30 minutes). Put 3 cups of sauce in a large baking pan. Place filets in sauce and cover with remaining sauce, cover pan and cook in oven for 12 minutes at 400 degrees. Put fish on place, top with 3 ounces of Hollandaise sauce and sprinkle with diced green onions.

**STORY & PHOTOGRAPHY
BY GARY N. ROSS, PH.D**

Gulf Fritillary

Whenever some species of animal is showcased, customarily only the adult form and usually a male at that, is depicted. For butterflies and other insects, the practice can be misleading. Consider the life cycle of a typical butterfly: egg — 3-to 6-day duration, larva or caterpillar —10-to 15-day duration, pupa or chrysalis — 10-to 15-day duration, and adult — 14-to 21-day duration. Obviously, an individual male butterfly — albeit the most handsome of all forms — is a relatively minor component in a complicated series of metamorphic stages.

The Gulf fritillary (*Agraulis vanillae*) is a medium-size butterfly belonging to a family of butterflies (Heliconiidae) commonly called heliconians or longwings. The 65 species within the family share the following characteristics: elongated wings, colorful, relatively slow flying, most frequently encountered within tropical zones, utilization of various species of passion vine (*Passiflora*) as host plants (plants on which females lay eggs), immunity from vertebrate predation because of distasteful body juices (caused by the sequestering of toxins acquired from passion vine during larval stages and from secretions from terminal abdominal glands released when the butterflies are alarmed), especially long lives (up to nine months) and relatively high intelligence that allows adults to learn the location of favorite nectar and host plants for repeated visitation.

Various components of both the common and scientific names reveal much about this species of butterfly. "Gulf,"indicates that the butterflies are found commonly throughout the Gulf coast states (in fact, the Gulf fritillary is the only longwing that breeds consistently in temperate regions); "fritillary" is from the Latin *fritillus*, meaning "dice cup" and refers to checkered dice-like markings (black on top, silver below) on the wings (there are many species of butterflies with "fritillary" as part of their name, but all belong to another family). "*Agraulis*" is based on the Latin root *agro* or *agri*, meaning field, grassy or country area, and describes the butterflies' preference for open habitats such as roadsides, meadows and flowery urban areas; "*vanillae*" is derived from *Vanilla*, an orchid genus, and alludes to the sweetish odor produced by abdominal scent glands of both males and females.

Life Cycle

Female butterflies deposit yellow eggs singly on the new leaves and tendrils of blue-flowered *Passiflora incarnata* (often called maypop) and the yellow-flowered *P. lutea*. Both host plants are common throughout Louisiana.

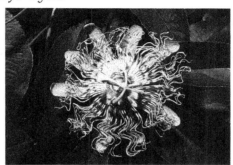

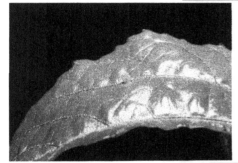

Within a few days tiny larvae emerge and begin feeding. The crawlers are glossy black with prominent orange stripes. In addition, larvae possess long, branched black spines that, although formidable looking, are completely harmless to humans. (Keep in mind that no butterfly larva is capable of stinging or biting.)

The caterpillars feed voraciously and shed (molt) their skins five times during their 10- to 14-day growth. Since a single passion vine may support many larvae, a given plant usually becomes defoliated — but not killed — during the caterpillars' maturation.

When fully grown, about 2 inches in length, a caterpillar locates a reasonably rigid structure, often a considerable distance — as great as 85 feet — from the host plant. There it attaches its rear with a silken button spun from silk glands located in its head, and hangs head downward to metamorphose. After a day or two, the skin splits revealing a mottled tan pupa or chrysalis. Resembling a dried, rolled leaf, the chrysalis hangs camouflaged from predators for 8 to 11 days. Then, the skin splits again and the butterfly emerges, expands, dries its wings, and finally takes to the air. Mating occurs soon after (sometimes before the female has even taken flight), and eggs are laid within a day or two to begin another generation. Adults live between four and five weeks, and are able to complete five to eight reproduction cycles before winter.

Adults are not cold tolerant and do not migrate. However, during some autumns, thousands of Gulf fritillaries can be observed in coastal areas such as Grand Isle and Cameron as they fly toward the west and southwest — presumably to the warmer regions of south Texas and northern Mexico. There are even records of Gulf fritillaries landing on ships and petroleum rigs and platforms nearly 75 miles offshore in the Gulf of Mexico. These fall emigrants do not return in the spring.

Most Gulf fritillaries, however, simply remain in Louisiana until the first hard freeze of winter. They quickly die from the cold or soon starve to death. On the other hand, larvae are less sensitive to cold. They are usually able to complete their feeding — even consuming frost damaged vegetation, transform into chrysalides and then remain in a prolonged pupal stage until the warmth of spring. They then emerge to begin the first generation of the new season. For those gardeners wishing to attract butterflies to their home turf, a generous planting of lantana and passion vine will surely guarantee the continued presence of one of nature's "dancing flowers," the lovely Gulf fritillary.

Nutria Itch

Photo by Leo Quebedeaux

Scourge of the Marsh

BY ANDY CRAWFORD

Danny Felterman was gathering alligator eggs in the summer of 1992. The weather was hot and much of the marsh water through which he waded was stagnant. The water helped cool him, however, so he didn't worry with wearing rubber boots or waders.

The relief was deceptive. The waters were being prowled by an unseen invader that causes that great coastal irritation, nutria itch.

Only a few minutes after visiting one nest, Felterman began to feel a sharp stinging around his ankles. Within minutes the stinging changed to an intense itching and a rash began to appear around his ankles. Felterman, who had watched nutria itch in action on a friend, knew almost instantly that he was in for a rough couple of weeks.

The intense discomfort of this malady has caused some coastal trappers to give up their trade. With proper care and attention the risk of contracting nutria itch can be greatly reduced.

Historically, trappers and other coastal residents were most likely to contract the parasite causing nutria itch. The rash, shown in the bottom photo, is normally a maze of elongated lesions beginning at the lower extremities and moving toward the torso. In extreme cases, the rash can even reach the victim's face.

During the next few days, the itch became almost unbearable. "I scratched my ankles so much I almost peeled the skin off," the 44-year-old Patterson resident said. "The more I scratched the worse it got."

Paul Coreil of the LSU Cooperative Extension Service said anyone who has had the misfortune of suffering from a red bug infestation has experienced a similar, though much shorter, irritation. "You can take the worst case of red bug itch and it just persists," Coreil said.

The rash spreads upward as the itch intensifies. Coreil, who has suffered from the malady three times, is quite familiar with this movement of the rash from lower extremities to the torso. "The only way you know it's nutria itch is the movement of the rash," he said. "It moves to the torso and eventually dies in the body."

The rash does not take a certain shape, but its indicative movement is obvious. "It can run from bumps the size of pimples to a long rash — almost a jagged line," Felterman explained.

Itching can be so severe that sleep can be affected. "Some people I talked with couldn't sleep because it was so bad," said Dr. Dale Little of Tulane University School of Medicine's Department of Tropical Medicine and Public Health. Little has worked with nutria itch since the late 1960s.

The exact parasite causing nutria itch is

isms leave the feces and burrow through the clothing and then the skin of the unfortunate trapper or hunter and moves just below the skin's surface, causing the symptomatic rash and intense itching.

There are other areas throughout the country where similar conditions are known by different names. "It may be called clam digger's itch, swimmer's itch or rice patty itch in other parts of the country," said Baton Rouge dermatologist Lloyd H. Frye. "I'm sure there are multiple other names that it could go by."

The condition is fairly well known and easily recognized in coastal areas. Little said that, in years past, trap-

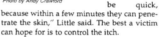

Photo by Andy Crawford

pers have been most affected by the malady. "Some of them reacted so badly they had to give up trapping and going into the marshes," he said.

But those who contract the parasite while temporarily visiting the coast can be confounded because medical personnel outside these regions rarely recognize the condition.

Treatment for the malady is not absolutely essential, since the parasite dies, itching ceases and the rash disappears without after effects in seven to 10 days. The severity and length of infection can be lessened, however, through treatment with prescription drugs such as Mintozol and Celestone.

"They're toxins that you take to kill the parasite," Coreil said. The medicine is taken orally and used as a lotion on affected areas.

These drugs can, however, have side effects. "I don't like them because they make me nauseous and irritable," Coreil said.

Treatment with antihistamines can help with the itching.

Protection against the skin-boring parasite is difficult. Felterman said he has found no effective means of avoiding nutria itch short of staying out of the water. "I even went so far as to make a vinyl apron, but I still caught it," he said.

Little said the only way to stop infection is by wearing chest waders or rubber boots extending above the water. "These larvae are so small they can migrate right through damp cloth," he explained.

The poor unfortunate who ventures into *Strongyloides*-infested waters without protection suffers quickly. "You know almost immediately," Perry said. "Just a few minutes later you start feeling a tingling."

At that point preventative measures are almost impossible. "It would have to be quick, because within a few minutes they can penetrate the skin," Little said. The best a victim can hope for is to control the itch.

LDWF biologist Mike Windham said he showered within two hours of falling in stagnant marsh water, but still developed the symptomatic rash. He was fortunate enough, however, not to suffer from the intense itching that usually accompanies the rash.

Felterman said his one stroke of luck is that itching has lessened with each episode. Little, however, said that Felterman is the exception. "The repeat infection may be more pronounced," he said. "I think it depends upon the interval between episodes. If there's a long delay it might be worse."

The bottom line is precaution. If working, fishing, hunting or trapping in stagnant, heavily vegetated coastal waters during warm months, make every effort to stay out of the water. Keep a pair of chest waders just in case wading around is necessary. They may be uncomfortable and hot, but that short-term discomfort is much easier to bear than 10 days of unbearable itching. ⌇

It is wise to give wide berth to stagnant water, as these areas are where the parasite causing nutria itch is most likely to be encountered.

Photo by Andy Crawford

The Gulf's CRIMSON Beauties

BY CHRIS BERZAS

Somewhere 35 miles south of Vermilion Bay and Southwest Pass, the *Bottom Line* anchored in the Gulf of Mexico near an oil rig.

Dr. Jeff LaBorde of Lafayette, captain of our crew, was quite optimistic about our location, and eight guest anglers quickly baited sharpened hooks with portions of squid.

It didn't take long for a few triggerfish to grab our offerings, but we waited patiently for our real quarry to begin feeding.

Sure enough, the fish were there and succumbed to our efforts. And it was true fun, especially when fishing in 60 to 70 feet of water, your rod buckling in an effort to keep up with the solid, steady runs of these brute fish.

Most of the anglers were fishing with Garcia 7600 reels attached to stout saltwater Ugly Stiks. Fifty-pound test Ande monofilament and test shock leaders with ball weights attached completed our outfits.

Rods arched and reels hummed as we fought and kept nearly a limit of fish per angler on that fine April day. It was time well spent, especially when admiring these radiant, crimson denizens of the deep. Moreover, we had managed to harvest some of the tastiest flesh that ever lay as a slab on the sides of any finned skeleton in the entire Gulf of Mexico.

Red snapper (*Lutjanus campechanus*) is certainly a beloved saltwater species inhabiting the depths along our coast. Prized for their tasty flesh, these fish are rated in the top 10 in terms of the most sought after species by Louisiana saltwater anglers.

For the novice to the behavioral characteristics of this species, it can't be overstated that red snappers have a fond affinity for structure. By structure, of course we're referring to the scores of rigs and reefs found past the green and blue water lines of the Gulf.

According to Harry Blanchet, Acting Finfish · Programs Manager with the Louisiana Department of Wildlife and Fisheries (LDWF), these red brutes are groupies indeed, in that they have a tendency to move in schools adjacent to structure. They range over the entire Gulf and can be found in depths as shallow as 25 feet, They are more readily found in depths of 40- to 60-feet.

"Most of the time, you won't catch them in water shallower than 60 feet," said Blanchet. "They're just not abundant at those depths and that's chiefly due to salinity levels in Louisiana. They prefer salinity levels at 30-parts per thousand."

In terms of size, these fish can reach 30-inches in length and weigh 30 pounds or more. Currently, the Louisiana State Fish Records as kept by the Louisiana Outdoor Writers Association shows the top-ranked red snapper to have weighed 39.1-pounds. It was taken by James F. Tomeny in June of 1994.

Prior to the mid-1980s these fish were plentiful. The only major obstacles facing anglers intent on catching these delicacies were the winds and high seas.

"We faced a real decline in numbers of this species until the mid-1980s," said Blanchet.

"By 1985, anglers were crying 'no more snappers' in the traditional fishing areas in the Gulf."

Sure enough, regulations were then implemented. The use of commercial long-lines for this species was belatedly prohibited and in November 1984, a minimum commercial size limit was set at 12 inches fork length. There was no recreational creel limit save for five fish less than 12 inches per person.

In 1990, a commercial reef fishing permit was mandated and the minimum size limit was increased to 14 inches. Recreational anglers were still restricted to a seven fish bag limit. In that same year, the annual commercial quota was set at 3.1 million pounds, and reduced to 2.04 million pounds for the 1992 season. It was then increased to 3.06-million pounds in 1993 under a red snapper endorsement system for the entire Gulf.

In 1995, the recreational minimum size was increased to 15 inches forked length, and the creel was reduced to a five-fish bag limit in both state and federal waters. According to Blanchet, the minimum size limit for red snappers taken commercially in Louisiana was increased to 15 inches total length just this past February in keeping with federal regulations.

The present goal for red snappers as envisioned by the Gulf of Mexico Fishery Management Council is to have stocks back to where they need to be by the year 2009. The massive loss of juvenile snapper in the shrimp bycatch is a major concern along with careful monitoring of the 6 million pound quota shared almost equally between commercial and recreational anglers.

Most recreational snapper anglers will attest that the management plan appears to be working. Apparently, the average size of this species has increased in the recreational catch, and most anglers find little difficulty catching a limit of 4- to 10-pound fish.

"I've never seen so many 30-pounders as we see now," said LaBorde. "In the last eight years, the larger fish have become plentiful. We've even changed our techniques to catch them with bigger reels (10,000 series 4/0), and we also employ drift fishing with a locked drag.

"The drag's locked because the bigger fish have a tendency to head straight to the pilings under the rigs where they can break off," added LaBorde. "The first one to two minutes can become critical, and if we can hold them then, we have a better chance of taking them."

LaBorde fishes year round for this species and targets various sizes of the fish. The angler contends that it isn't unusual to find small to medium fish nearer the bottom, while the larger snappers tend to suspend somewhat higher.

Regarding tackle, LaBorde will chiefly use the heavy equipment noted above. He vertically drops squid or cigar minnows attached to a 6/0 hook on nylon leaders.

"Snappers are chiefly an olfactory species in terms of finding food," said LaBorde. "Artificial lures are hardly used to catch these fish."

LaBorde is concerned with the future availability of cigar minnows due to the newly enacted Act 1316 passed during the 1995 session of the Louisiana Legislature. Changes in commercial netting regulations may increase the cost of such bait.

"We are looking at various other species besides cigar minnows to use as bait," LaBorde said. "Pogeys, Spanish sardines and a host of other small species are now used when red snapper fishing."

However, some of us will use traditional bassin' equipment for the moderately sized red snapper. Nylon leaders and a loose drag are necessary when angling with relatively light equipment due to the initial brutish runs of the fish. Fishing in this manner can be quite fun due to the time it takes to battle these fish to the net or gaff. A caveat is due simply because an angler never knows when another large finned species will grab the bait and run hard resulting in snapped lines and/or broken equipment.

A recreational bag limit of five snappers might leave Louisiana anglers worried if a trip offshore is really worth the trouble. However, Blanchet contends that although both recreational and commercial anglers are seeing more and more restrictions, many recreational anglers on such trips target other species besides snappers such as king and Spanish mackerel, cobia, amberjack or even spotted seatrout.

As for the future of this species, only time will tell if Louisiana anglers will ever see them again in numbers experienced prior to the mid-1980s. However, pursuing these crimson denizens of the deep continues to be a celebrated legacy in Louisiana. ✦

Over-fishing once threatened the availability of red snapper in Louisiana waters. This favored species once again thrives around the many offshore oil rigs and reefs because of restrictions placed on harvest.

T<small>HE</small> J<small>OYS</small> & P<small>ITFALLS</small> <small>OF</small>
TRAILERING

CONDENSED FROM A PUBLICATION BY BOAT U./S.

oating on a highway, like boating on the water, requires some attentiveness. Boats go aground in the water. Boats can also "go aground" on a highway. Negotiating stoplights, potholes, slick spots and heavy vacation traffic while towing a cumbersome trailer and boat takes practice. Trailers, like boats, require TLC to keep them rolling.

Keeping Your Trailer Healthy

Three things dictate how often a trailer needs to be inspected: where it is used; how often it is used; and how hard it is used. A fourth consideration, just to complicate the discussion, might be the quality of the trailer itself. As a bare-bones minimum, any trailer should be thoroughly inspected at the start of each boating season. If a trailer is going to be used frequently, it will be dunked in saltwater and spend many hours traveling bumpy roads, you'll want to inspect key components more often. Here are a few tips and suggestions.

Frame and Axle

Submersible trailers are easier to use, but they also require more upkeep, especially when used in saltwater. Any rust on the frame should be sanded and re-painted or re-galvanized. If a structural component appears to be badly rusted, the trailer shouldn't be used until it is examined by an expert or the component is replaced. To prevent rust, even a galvanized trailer should be promptly rinsed after being dunked in saltwater.

Any loose nuts on the frame must be tightened. Structural component fastenings should be inspected frequently until you're confident none

are prone to loosening. Even the tightest trailer should be examined routinely on long trips.

Trailer Tires

A blown tire can be far more than an inconvenience. According to insurance claim files, tires are the most frequent cause of trailer failure, and broken axles and spilled boats can result. Treads should be examined before the trailer is used, but keep in mind that most trailer tires die of old age. A likely indication of impending trouble is spider web cracks on the sidewall, which indicate the tire is rotten. While you're examining the sidewalls, take a look at the wheel lugs to make sure they're tight.

Check the maximum load limit printed on the sidewalls. If there are two tires rated for 1,000 pounds each, the total weight of the boat, the trailer and all gear should be no more than 2,000 pounds.

Trailer tires often suffer from under inflation and should be checked whenever the trailer is used. Correct tire pressures are also stamped on the sidewall. Underinflated tires build up heat, which can cause the layers (plies) inside the tire to delaminate. Sudden tire failure is the result.

Spare Tires, Hassles and Theft

Considering what is at stake, it is surprising how many boaters do not carry a spare tire for their trailers. Trying to find someone who can fix a flat or replace a blown tire can be a hassle, to say the least. There is also a considerable risk that while you're searching for a gas station, someone will steal the boat. A boater in Texas left his boat and trailer to get a tire repaired and returned later to find his outboard missing. Leaving again to report the theft to police, he returned and found the boat and trailer (and most of his luggage) had also disappeared. Note: The typical car jack will not work on a trailer. You'll need to get a scissors jack or hydraulic jack large enough to handle the load.

Hubs

When you arrive at the launch, allow time for the hubs to cool. Otherwise, cold water can be drawn into the bearings, causing rust. Bearing protectors, which are caps with springs that hold grease under pressure, are an excellent investment that virtually eliminates water penetration into the hub or the formation of condensation. Keep protectors properly filled with an approved trailer wheel bearing grease at all times.

boat's stern to the trailer. If a strap isn't used, the boat will bounce against (or off) the trailer. And don't rely on the winch cable to secure the bow. Use a separate strap from the bow eye down to the trailer frame.

Successful Towing

Five to 10 percent of the total weight of the boat, motor, trailer and gear should be on the trailer ball when the coupler is parallel to the ground. Too much weight on the ball will make the car difficult to steer. (And good luck when you're launching your boat at a steep launch ramp, especially if your car has front-wheel drive.) Too little weight on the ball and the trailer is apt to fishtail. Weight can be moved by shifting the boat on the trailer or by moving the trailer's axle backward or forward as required.

Hitches and Couplings

Trailer hitches are rated in four classes according to the gross weight they will be pulling. The weight of your boat, trailer and gear should never exceed hitch capacity.

Safety Chains

Always use a safety chain criss-crossed between the car and the trailer coupling. Should all else fail, the chain will keep the trailer from flying off the road. Criss-crossing the chain prevents the trailer coupler from dropping to the road. Leave enough slack to allow for proper turning, but not so much that the chain drags. A shackle/pin is far more secure than the standard S-hook.

Towing a Trailer

The first thing you should remember when you tow a trailer is that you are towing a trailer. When the car is humming merrily along, it is easy to forget the trailer is back there. Slow down! Slower speeds are safer and will reduce the strain on your car and trailer. Swing wider at corners. The trailer's wheels are closer to the inside on turns than the wheels of the tow vehicle. Braking is also affected, so leave extra distance between you and the car ahead of you. And remember to allow extra space when you pass other cars.

On trips, check the wheel hubs every time you stop. If one or both feel abnormally hot, the bearings should be inspected before you continue. Lug nuts on the wheels and nuts and bolts on the trailer frame should also be examined to make sure they're tight.

Launching the Boat

If the ramp is crowded (and it usually is on weekends), prepare your boat and trailer before it is your turn to launch. Raise the lower unit, install the drain plug, release the securing straps, and disconnect the trailer lights. If you are stepping a mast, make sure there are no power-lines between you and the ramp.

To a beginner, backing a trailer down a ramp can be like standing on your head and reading a book in a mirror. It takes practice. Learning can be rough on the blood pressure — yours and the other people waiting patiently (or impatiently) to launch their boats. Better to practice backing the trailer in the quiet safety of your driveway. Tip: push the bottom of the car's steering wheel in the direction you want the car to go.

Use your car's parking brake, keep a tire stop handy, and leave the car's engine running in case you need power quickly. That may seem elementary, but more than one boater has watched truck and trailer roll backward down the ramp to disappear beneath the water. That makes for a long walk home.

Louisiana's Official Wildlife & Fisheries Posters *

*Actual poster size 17"

After four years, the Department of Wildlife & Fisheries has republished its seven popular posters. Depicted stunning color are the snakes, waterfowl, fish, amphibians and turtles of Louisiana. Suitable for framing, th can be enjoyed by the whole family. Buy them singly or by the set!

Set includes:

Common Saltwater Fish	Common Freshwater Fish	Snakes of Louisiana	Waterfowl of Louisiana
Common Offshore Fish		Turtles of Louisiana	Amphibians of Louisiana

---

	Quantity	Price Each	Total
Common Offshore Fish			
Common Freshwater Fish			
Common Saltwater Fish			
Amphibians of Louisiana			
Turtles of Louisiana			
Snakes of Louisiana			
Waterfowl of Louisiana			
		Subtotal	$
**Tax (4% state tax, EBR residents add add'l 4% tax)			$
		Shipping & handling	$3.00
		Total amount due	$

Price List (any combination)

1-2 posters	*$4.00 each*
3-6 posters	*$3.50 each*
7 or more	*$3.00 each*

Method of Payment

☐ Check/Money order   ☐ MasterCard   ☐ VI

Credit card information:
Account number_____
Expiration date_____
Signature_____

Ship to:
Name_____
Address_____
City_____ State _____ Zip _____
Phone (_____)_____

Mail to:
Louisiana Conservationist
P.O. Box 98000
Baton Rouge, LA 70898
504/765-2918

NOCTURNAL ANIMALS

BY AMY OUCHLEY & GAY BRANTLEY

LOUISIANA

NATURE INVESTIGATION

et's investigate some of nature's activity at night. If you have ever kept a hamster as a pet, then you know the meaning of nocturnal. A hamster is **nocturnal, active during the night**. Animals **active during the day** are **diurnal**.

What are some more examples of nocturnal animals? Owls, bats, fireflies, and flying squirrels are nocturnal. They have special features that allow them to feed, find a mate, and move during the night. These special features are called adaptations.

Nocturnal Adaptations

Owl - large eyes, sensitive ears, special feathers for quiet flying.
Bat - only mammal with wings, large ears, uses echolocation.
Firefly - flashes light signals.
Flying Squirrel - large eyes, sensitive ears, sensitive whiskers.

Directions

Connect the dots to find an animal that uses its keen sense of hearing to find prey at night. Special feathers allow this animal to fly quietly.

Word Search

Find and circle the words hidden in this puzzle.

```
I  Q  J  A  S  E  S  S  C  H  J  S  T  U  T
F  O  N  F  C  I  S  D  O  O  T  V  E  Y  D
L  E  S  E  M  E  F  T  O  T  I  E  N  A  E
W  Q  Y  R  N  O  H  I  P  V  V  D  A  A  Z
O  E  A  K  E  G  T  X  R  H  S  U  N  R  F
S  A  R  D  I  H  N  H  T  E  F  T  K  V  S
L  A  F  L  A  O  T  O  G  A  F  D  A  N  O
D  O  I  G  D  P  T  A  C  I  G  L  I  R  N
T  W  D  D  N  T  T  A  E  T  L  U  Y  D  S
T  A  A  G  L  S  H  A  B  F  U  N  C  A  T
C  W  K  V  J  W  K  G  T  G  I  R  O  J  C
N  L  X  I  G  A  O  S  I  I  F  K  N  O  L
N  W  J  U  V  A  U  I  U  N  O  E  G  A  M
O  D  I  U  R  N  A  L  U  D  S  N  B  C  L
M  W  I  P  M  O  E  K  F  B  B  Z  S  Z  P
```

ADAPTATIONS
MOONLIGHT
BAT
MOTH
DARKNESS
NIGHT
DAWN
NOCTURNAL
DIURNAL
OWL
DUSK
STARS
EARS
TWILIGHT
EYES
FEATHERS
FIREFLY

Hone Your Senses

When you go outside at night, think about using all your senses to investigate. Listen for different frogs or insects that call at night. Follow a firefly and count the number of flashes it makes in one minute. Watch for bats catching insects at dusk. Touch a tree to feel its bark. Sniff the odors of the night. Now you are becoming a real nature investigator.

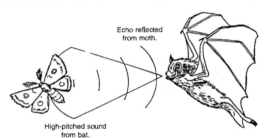

Echo reflected from moth.

High-pitched sound from bat.

Glossary

Adaptations - special features in organisms that result from adjusting to a specific environment.

Echolocation - high-pitched sounds produced by some animals, such as bats, which bounce off nearby objects and return to their ears as echoes.

Mate - the male or female of a pair of animals.

the four-point buck hanging from a tree nearby. Only then does one of the silent threesome respond to the officer's questions.

The deer was killed early in the afternoon and none of them had left the camp after dark according to the spokesman, who answers bluntly between long pulls on a beer can. The blood and the warm, limber carcass of the deer contest the poacher's statements but the officer will need more than "It was warm and limber, your honor!" if he is to successfully convict these violators.

Thanks to training recently received by the Department of Wildlife and Fisheries Enforcement Division this agent will be able to cite and successfully convict these outlaws.

Referred to as time of death or TOD, the forensic study of chemical and physical changes in the carcass of a deer following death provides data admissible in court. TOD techniques are not new. Studies in Maine, Illinois, Virginia, Indiana, Nebraska and Pennsylvania have been under way since as far back as 1965. In February 1996, two officers from the Pennsylvania Game Commission came to Louisiana and taught a three-day class on TOD technique. They used methods described by David W. Oates, wildlife forensic and analytic specialist with the Nebraska Game and Parks Commission, in the *Wildlife Forensic Field Manual*, a publication of the Association of Midwest Fish and Game Law Enforcement Officers.

According to Oates, TOD has been estimated by several techniques with temperature measurements and response to electrical stimulus being the most reliable. Monitoring chemical and physical changes in the eye and the rigor mortis sequence can also be of value.

Temperature readings on a cooling deer carcass are predictable and reliable providing the officer with a way to determine how long the animal has been dead. The ambient or air temperature for the first 12 hours after death and the weight of the deer are needed. Using thermometers to take temperature readings at the thigh and in nasal passages, the officer can collect data which is compared to cooling rate charts and thus determine TOD.

Response to electrical stimulus is chemically related to the availability of adenosine triphosphate (ATP) in muscles. After death ATP breaks down and response to electrical stimulus gradually decreases until no response is observed. The value of this test is its ability to allow TOD estimates for the first few hours (four or less) after death. The test can be conducted with a 10 foot length of 14 gauge double insulated wire, alligator clamps and a vehicle. The vehicles distributor cap is the energy source. Electricity is then applied to several muscle groups and the response is recorded.

Several interesting phenomena occur in the eye following death, also aiding TOD estimates. Loss of eye clarity, changes in luminosity and shape, color changes in the pupil and constriction of the pupil are all TOD indicators. Pupil constriction can be photographed so that a permanent visible record is available for court. Again, recorded information is compared to known data.

Rigor mortis is familiar to everyone. It is defined as a post mortem state of rigidity which develops in muscle tissue when ATP and phosphocreatine has been depleted. Depletion takes place via a chemical reaction and depends on physiology and ambient temperature. A fairly reliable rigor sequence has been derived for deer. By gently attempting to flex selected joints in their normal plane of movement, the officer can determine the stage of rigor and the length of time since death.

Determining TOD in white-tailed deer represents yet another advance in the professional abilities of Louisiana's wildlife enforcement agents. Through exchange of information and cooperation with wildlife officers in other states we can move conservation law enforcement to a degree of efficiency that will create a deterrent in the minds of potential violators.

From time to time we will discuss other new training and techniques implemented in the enforcement of Louisiana's fish and game regulations. We must continue to train and seek new knowledge in order to effectively protect our wildlife resources.

LDWF Continues to Stock Florida Strain Bass

As many as 350,000 Florida large-mouth bass fingerlings were stocked in south Louisiana waterways in April. Biologists from the Department of Wildlife and Fisheries, in conjunction with Dow Chemical and Louisiana Bass Hatcheries, stocked Lac Des Allemands, Ruddock Canal and the Tangipahoa and Tickfaw river systems.

The stocking project is entering its fourth year of a commitment by the Department to bass fishermen whose fisheries were affected by Hurricane Andrew. As part of the agreement, fingerlings will be stocked in areas where fishing pressure increased as a result of habitat losses due to the storm.

Stocking actually begins with production of fingerlings from well-selected brood stock. Biologists began the week of Feb. 12, 1996, preparing a pond at Dow Chemical's Plaquemine plant, where 75 pairs of adult Florida largemouth bass will be spawned. The fish from the Department's Beechwood hatchery in Forest Hill will be placed in the pond in early March. These adult fish will be returned to state hatcheries when spawning is completed.

Stocking was completed by the end of April. Inch-long fingerlings were netted and placed in large holding tanks for transport. The fish were then motored to selected sites and released.

More than 500,000 bass fingerlings from the Dow Chemical pond have been stocked in the Atchafalaya Basin and other areas in south Louisiana during the past three years.

LDWF Utilizes Federal Funds to Enhance Reforestation

More than 23,000 hardwood seedlings were planted on 120 acres of state-owned land in DeSoto Parish on Feb. 13-14, 1996, as part of the Department of Wildlife and Fisheries' ongoing efforts to return marginal croplands to native bottomland-hardwood forests. Seedlings were supplied by the National Tree Trust, an entity that develops partnerships between the timber and paper industry, governmental agencies and volunteer citizen groups to enhance forests.

The 1-year-old seedlings were placed on the northern end of Bayou Pierre Wildlife Management Area. The Department is developing Bayou Pierre into a recreational area for small game hunters.

The National Tree Trust (NTT) was enacted by Congress in 1990 through a one-time grant to promote volunteerism and create an awareness of the importance of maintaining the nation's forests. The group's goals include a 10-year initiative to plant 30 million trees. Since operations began, NTT has partnered with more than 500 volunteer groups in 45 states to plant more than 2.5 million trees.

Although seedlings were provided through the National Tree Trust, they originated from seven timber and paper companies headquartered across the southeastern United States: Georgia-Pacific Corp., Kimberly Clark Corp., Westvaco Corp., Louisiana-Pacific Corp., Temple-Inland Corp., Mill Creek Farm and International Paper.

OGT Names Winners

Operation Game Thief, Louisiana's grassroots anti-poaching organization, announced winners of a drawing held at its annual meeting in Baton Rouge last January.

Russell Richard of Lafayette won a 10-gauge double-barreled shotgun and Jay Guidry of Opelousas took home a 12-gauge pump.

OGT raised more than $1,500 for rewards through fundraising. Money

Lifetime Licenses

Bamber, III., James E.	Prairieville
Book, Jr., Napoleon	Tallulah
Braud, Charles E.	Prairieville
Chambers, III., Lawrence	Greenwell Sprgs.
Cornell, Douglas E.	Baton Rouge
Dinger, III., Henry J.	Lake Charles
Efferson, Malcom C.	Livingston
Foret, David M.	Galliano
Fremin, Joachim R.	New Iberia
Guitreau, Joshua J.	Maurepas
Guy, Samuel J.	Mansfield
Harrington, David G.	Plaquemine
Harris, Eric J.	Bastrop
Harris, Odis C.	Bastrop
Hoenke, Amanda W.	Minden
Horton, Douglas T.	Montegut
Mashburn, Willis F.	Zachary
Meachum, Jr., Dale C.	Downsville
Norman, IV., Ernest B.	New Orleans
Robertson, Charles P.	Tickfaw
Sanders, Shannon Dale	Kentwood
Simon, Carey P.	Lake Arthur
West, Hampton G.	Baton Rouge
Williams, Justin C.	Baton Rouge
Williams, M. Reid	Baton Rouge
Williams, M. Travis	Baton Rouge
Arellano, Anthony R.	Madisonville
Beaird, Christopher E.	Shreveport
Beaird, Janet R.	Shreveport
Bonneval, Beau G.	Thibodaux
Bordelon, Christopher	Pine Prairie
Bordelon, Jr., William	Boyce
Boyer, Jack A.	Lake Charles
Boyer, Sam H.	Lake Charles
Brackin, Marshall L.	Baton Rouge
Bridges, Matthew W.	Monroe
Champagne, Jeff S.	Thibodeaux
Correro, Michael A.	West Monroe
Crain, Jr., Jeffrey L.	Shreveport
Dupre', Seth J.	Arnaudville
Dupre', Taylor P.	Arnaudville
Dupre', William L.	Arnaudville
Eaves, Robert S.	Baton Rouge
Fontenot, Jeffery W.	Youngsville
Hamby, Brent M.	Monroe
Kenwright, Joe	Monroe
Lagneaux, Ryan J.	Carencro
Landry, Jarett M.	New Iberia
Markham, Randall T.	Ruston
Meadows, John E.	Dubach
Morgan, Dennis M.	Many
Newton, Jeffery J.	Batchelor
O'Connor, David J.	Scott
Parker, Matthew J.	Houma
Radford, John W.	Lake Charles
Ramie, David P.	Lake Charles
Reid, II., Charles M.	Amite
Sehon, Brenda G.	Junction City
Sexton, Jr., John W.	Rosepine
Valentine, Jacob M.	Gonzales
Valentine, Joshua W.	Gonzales
Aguillard, Kevin P.	Elton
Barrious, Joseph A.	Westwego
Becnel, Jr., Verney E.	St. Gabriel
Boyd, Tyler M.	Monroe
Butaud, Thomas R.	Opelousas
Carter. Allen A.	St. Bernard
Chatelain, Justin J.	Marksville
Cooper, Sr., Donald G.	Metairie
Cuccia, AAron M.	Harahan
Delee, Brent K.	Baton Rouge
Domingue, Dane L.	Rayne
Donahoe, Shamus P.	Welsh
Dupre, Glen P.	Grand Chenier
Elter, Stephanie G.	Fenton
Ewing, Arthur O.	New Roads
Ferran, Max G.	Metairie
Fisher, Alan D.	New Orleans
Gaston, Gregory C.	Sulphur
Gibson, Darryl W.	Prairieville
Gresham, Dean M.	Duson
Gresham, Michael K.	Lafayette
Gresham, Neil M.	Duson
Gresham, Ross G.	Duson
Hardie, Calvin K.	Metairie
Hearld, Jesse D.	Zachary
Herrington, Brad	Shreveport
Holloway, Brandon B.	Forest Hill
Johnson, Clint D.	Ruston
Kardorff, Archie E.	Metairie
Lafleur, Michael J.	Ville Platte
Laurent, J. Derek	Lafayette
Laurent, Travis P.	Lafayette
Lazenby, David P.	West Monroe
LeBouef, Kelly J.	Montegut
Ledoux, Richard L.	Livingston
Lumpkin, Kelly A.	Shreveport
Mannina, Glenn A.	Slidell
Mannina, Jason J.	Slidell
Mannina, Justin L.	Slidell
McManemin, Travis W.	Lake Charles
Merrell, Glen R.	Slidell
Mullins, John W.	Baton Rouge
Negron, Jorge J.	Ruston
Ortego, Brandon Keith	Pine Prairie
Ortego, Joseph E.	Pine Prairie
Preaus, Jacob H.	Farmerville
Reuther, Charles J.	Slidell
Roberts, James S.	Holden
Robicheaux, Jeremy P.	St. Martinville
Stafford, John M.	Baton Rouge
Stein, Austin C.	Laplace
Titus, Ill., Paul S.	Destrehan
Woodard, Sharon B.	Houma

CPSIA information can be obtained
at www.ICGtesting.com
Printed in the USA
BVHW041426241218
536331BV00015B/669/P

9 780266 589976